A NOTABLE LIFE SERIES

Madam C.J. Walker: *Inventor, Entrepreneur, Millionaire*

www.maryoluonye.com

Copyright © 2014 by Mary N. Oluonye. All rights reserved.

No part of this book may be reproduced, stored in a retrieval system, or transmitted by any means without the prior written permission of the author.

PHOTOS CREDITS:

A'Lelia Bundles/Madam Walker Family Archives,

www.madamcjwalker.com (portrait and products)

Istockphoto.com (maps, postcard, box)

U.S. Postal Service (postage stamp)

"Documenting the American South" http://docsouth.unc.edu, The University of North Carolina at Chapel Hill. (St. Paul A.M.E. Church, St. Louis, MO)

Library of Congress (plowing print)

ABOUT A NOTABLE LIFE SERIES

"Mary Oluonye brings Madam Walker's story to life in a way that will inspire young readers to follow their own dreams for success."

— A'Lelia Bundles, Madam Walker biographer
and great-great-grand-daughter

A Notable Life Series *reflects America's rich cultural diversity by introducing young readers to important, noteworthy historical and contemporary men and women of different ethnic heritages. Young readers get an overview of the person's life and learn how they were shaped by the circumstances and times in which they lived or live. Children gain an understanding of how these men and women set goals, faced challenges, and accomplished their goals through hard work, persistence and faith in themselves.*

For Teachers and Parents: *Free, downloadable Teacher Guides are available at* **www.maryoluonye.com**

Madam C.J. Walker

Born: December 23, 1867

Birthplace: Delta, Louisiana

Died: May 25, 1919

TABLE OF CONTENTS

The life of Madam C.J. Walker

Bibliography/Further Reading

Madam C.J. Walker

Inventor, Entrepreneur, Millionaire

1867 – 1919

Madam C.J. Walker's name at birth was Sarah Breedlove. She was born on December 23, 1867 in Delta, Louisiana. Her parents had six children. Sarah was their fifth child. Slavery had ended two years before Sarah Breedlove was born, and the Breedlove family was very poor, just like most newly freed black families living in the South were after the Civil War. Families

worked all day on farms. As soon as children were six or seven years old, they had to help out on the farm too. There was always a lot of hard work to do: plowing, planting, weeding, and taking care of animals too. Sarah also had to help out with household chores and laundry. Most Black children went to school for just two to five months a year. During the other months they were needed on the farm. Sarah, however, did not have a chance to go to school at all when she was a child.

By the time Sarah was seven years old, both of her parents were dead. It was now up to her older sister, Louvenia, to take care of both Sarah and her younger brother, Solomon. It was a struggle and life was very difficult.

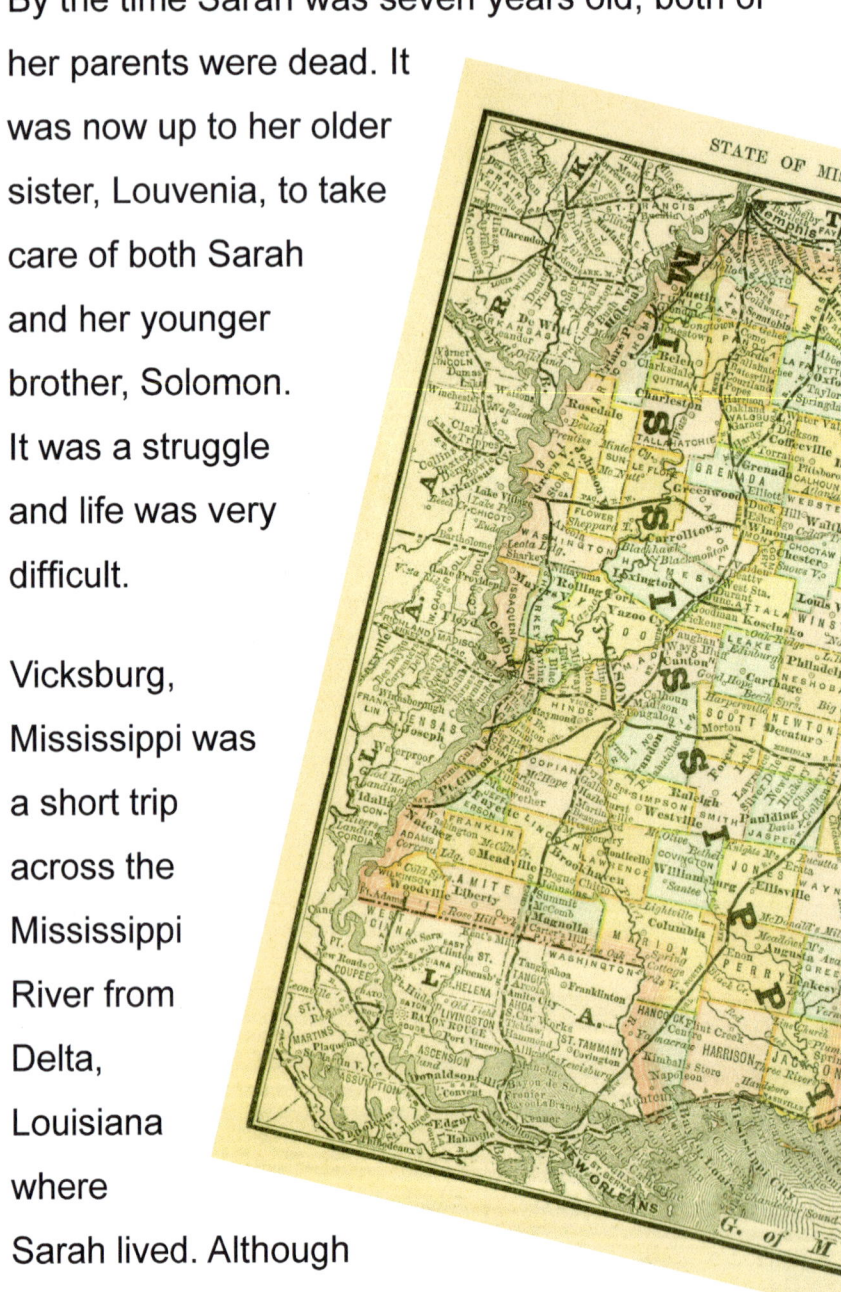

Vicksburg, Mississippi was a short trip across the Mississippi River from Delta, Louisiana where Sarah lived. Although people traveled easily between Delta and Vicksburg, many felt that there were more opportunities in Vicksburg. When Sarah was ten years old, they moved to Vicksburg, Mississippi where their older brothers were already living. When they arrived in Vicksburg, however, they found that there were not many jobs available. Louvenia eventually found a job washing clothes and Sarah helped her. But, when Louvenia got married, things took a turn for the worse for Sarah. She disliked the man her sister married. He was often angry and mean. Sarah desperately wanted to get away. So, when Moses McWilliams asked Sarah to marry him, she said, yes. She was only fourteen years old.

Three years later, Sarah gave birth to a baby girl. They named her, Lelia. Unfortunately, two years later, Sarah's husband died and suddenly, at the age of twenty, Sarah was a widow with a young child and very little money.

The word resilience means, "an ability to recover from or adjust easily to misfortune or change" (Merriam-Webster Dictionary). Sarah was a resilient young woman. By this time, her brothers had moved to St. Louis, Missouri and were working there as barbers. Sarah continued to work very hard and saved enough money so that by 1888, she was able to move to St. Louis. Like mothers everywhere,

 resilience an ability to recover from or adjust easily to misfortune or change 99

– *Merriam-Webster Dictionary*

Sarah wanted to make certain that her daughter had a greater chance for a better life, and St Louis seemed like the place to do it.

In St. Louis, Sarah's main goal was to take care of

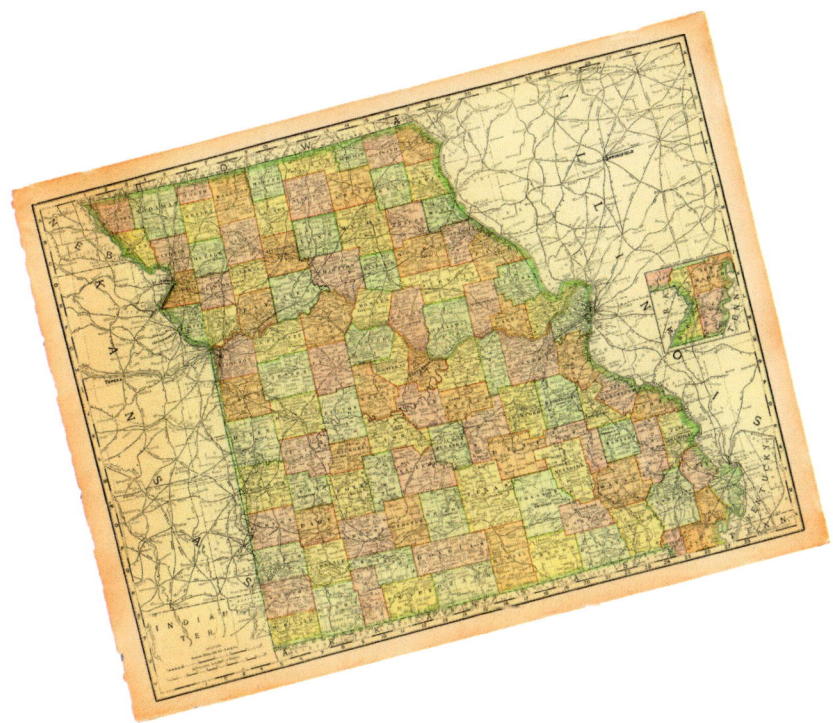

her daughter and make sure that she got a good education.

She had big plans for her daughter – college. In those days most Black women did not attend college. Sarah worked six days a week, washing other people's clothes in her home. She didn't make much money, but she was able to pay the bills and save a little each week to go toward Lelia's college fund. Sarah also managed to take a few night classes herself. While the focus was on working and

ST. PAUL A. M. E. CHURCH, ST. LO UIS, MO.

earning money, Sarah did have a little time to make friends, and she became involved in the thriving Black community and attended St. Paul A.M.E. (African Methodist Episcopal) Church. She also spent time with her brothers.

Working so hard for so long, along with all the stress

and poor eating habits affected Sarah. Her hair began to fall out. She searched store shelves for something to stop her hair loss, but nothing worked.

The products in stores were not made for African-American hair types. It was during this time that Sarah's entrepreneurial (business) spirit kicked in. She had a scalp and hair problem, and she noticed that she was not the only one with the problem. Also, there was no remedy available to her and the other women suffering with the same condition. What could she do? The solution came to her in a dream, she would later say. A man in her dream gave her a secret recipe to make hair grow. That was the start of Sarah's future business empire. Using the ingredients that had come to her in the dream, Sarah immediately began experimenting and eventually developed a scalp and hair formula. She tried it out on her own hair, and it worked! Next,

 She tried it out on her own hair, and it worked!

she tried it out on some of her friends' hair, and again, it worked.

Sarah knew she had a successful product that women would want, and more importantly, she had made a product that women would be willing to buy. She called her product, "Wonderful

Hair Grower," and went from house to house selling it (door-to-door sales).

Sarah devoted the next couple of years to taking the steps and making the decisions that would eventually lead to the creation of a highly successful national Black hair care company. She moved to Denver, Colorado in 1905 where she added the

finishing touches to her "Wonderful Hair Grower" formula, and developed several other products: Vegetable Shampoo; Glossine Hair Oil; Temple Salve; and Tetter Salve.

In 1906, Sarah married Charles Joseph Walker. It

was at this time that she took the name of Madam C.J. Walker and the name began to appear on all of her products. The two of them made a good team. With his experience in the newspaper business, they developed a new way to advertise and sell (distribute) products. They started a mail order department so that women across the country could buy Madam C.J. Walker products through the mail. The

company also started selling more and more products by working with many women. These Walker agents, as they were called, were trained in using the hair care products, dressed professionally and went door to door demonstrating and selling Walker's hair care products in their communities around the country.

This method of selling was a big success, and before too long almost one thousand women were working as independent agents with the company.

As agents, they worked on their own, selling Madam C.J. Walker company products. In return, the agents received a commission (a percentage of the price) on each product they sold. The agents made money and the Madam C.J. Company made money...a lot of money. Madam C.J. Walker and her husband would later get divorced, but she kept the same name.

In 1908, Madam C.J. Walker moved to Pittsburgh, Pennsylvania to start the Lelia College. The college was set up to train Black hair stylists on how to

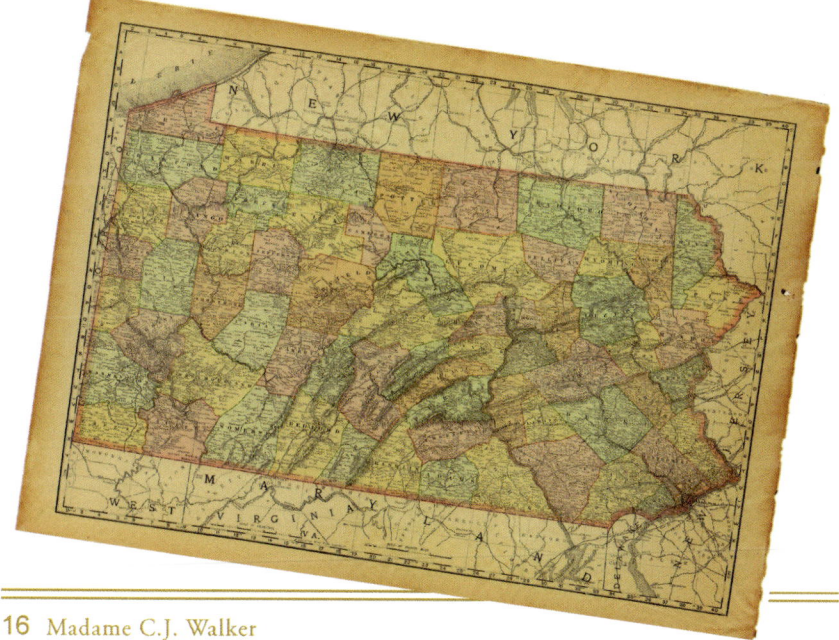

use the company products. Madam C.J. Walker's daughter, Lelia, was now involved in the business. At first, she was put in charge of running the mail order business in Denver. Later, she managed the Lelia College in Pittsburgh.

In 1910, Walker moved again – this time to Indianapolis, Indiana where she had the Madam C.J. Walker Manufacturing Company factory built.

She worked non-stop, continuing to travel all over the country, and to Central America and the Caribbean, selling products, making contacts and checking things out.

By 1918, Madam C.J. Walker was America's first female African-American self-made millionaire. Little Sarah Breedlove had come a long way. She

had created a new way of doing business and owned the largest Black business, and one or the largest women-owned businesses of her time. She amassed a fortune and made it possible for thousands of Black women to earn a living and start businesses of their own. Walker enjoyed spending some of the money she made on herself, but she was also a generous philanthropist. She donated money to Black colleges, the YMCA (Young Men's Christian Association), the National Association of Colored Women (NACW), and the National Association for the Advancement of Colored People (NAACP).

The years of unending hard work, stress and high blood pressure had taken their toll. On May 25, 1919, Madam C.J. Walker died in her home in New York. She was fifty-one years old.

Sarah Breedlove, also known as the famous, Madam C.J. Walker, grew up poor, and although she had limited formal education, she was a life-long learner. She hired a personal tutor when she needed to, and she became an avid reader. A brilliant thinker and creative problem solver, her inventions to help solve a common problem faced by many Black women improved thousands of lives.

Her company generated jobs, and made it possible for hundreds of people to earn a decent living. Madam C.J. Walker was a great role model then, and she is a great role model for today. She demonstrated the importance of having faith and confidence in yourself, using your mind to conceive ideas, make plans, and follow through on those plans.

Bibliography/Further Reading:

Bundles, A'Lelia. Madam C.J. Walker: Entrepreneur. New York: Chelsea House, 2008.

Camp, Carole. American Women Inventors. Berkeley Heights: Enslow Publishers, 2004.

Hobkirk, Lori. Journey to Freedom: Madam C.J. Walker. Mankato: Child's World, 2009.

Hudson, Wade. Black Heroes: Five Notable Inventors. New York: Scholastic, 1995.

Lasky, Kathryn. Vision of Beauty: The Story of Sarah Breedlove Walker. Cambridge: Candlewick Press, 2000.

McKissack, Fredrick & Patricia. Madam C.J. Walker: Self-Made Millionaire. Berkeley Heights: Enslow Publishers, 2001.

Website:

A'Lelia Bundles/Madam Walker Family Archives: www.madamcjwalker.com

Design: Janet Dodrill

Printed in Poland
by Amazon Fulfillment
Poland Sp. z o.o., Wrocław